Museums of the World

The Kunsthistorisches Museum Vienna

The Kunsthistorisches Museum Vienna

The Imperial and Ecclesiastical Treasury

Manfred Leithe-Jasper
and Rudolf Distelberger

C.H. Beck/Scala Books

FRONTISPIECE
**Emperor Charles VI (1685–1740) in the
robes of the Golden Fleece**
ascribed to Johann Gottfried Auerbach
(1697-1743)
Vienna about 1730;
Oil on canvas;
297x 196 cm
(Inv. No. GG 2140)
The Emperor points to the table with the insignia of his title,
the Austrian archducal coronet, the Bohemian Wenceslaus
crown, the imperial crown and the Hungarian crown of St
Stephen.

Front cover illustration:
The Emperor Rudolf II's crown, (see page 14)

Back cover illustration:
The imperial crown, detail: enamel plate with
King David (see page 48)

Photography: Kunsthistorisches Museum, Vienna
Layout: Sara Robin, London
Editing: Verlag C.H. Beck, Munich
and Scala Books, London
Translated into English by Dinah Livingstone
Translation Consultant: Mag. Barbara Rambousek,
Staatlich Geprüfter Fremdenführer, Austria

© 2003 Scala Publishers, London/
Verlag C.H. Beck, Munich

First published in 1998 by
Scala Publishers
Northburgh House, 10 Northburgh Street
London EC1V 0AT

Sale of the German edition
in Germany, Austria and Switzerland:
Verlag C.H.Beck, Munich

ISBN 3 406 42938 6

Printed in Italy by Giunti Industrie Grafiche

Contents

Introduction

The Vienna treasury is rightly called the cradle of the imperial collections, as it goes back to the medieval family treasure of the house of Hapsburg. Although we only have a sketchy knowledge of the family or household treasure belonging to individual branches of the medieval Hapsburg family, some sources do give us information about what it once contained, and some individual objects still held in the Kunsthistorisches Museum today can be traced back to the early Fifteenth Century. Even early on, efforts were made to keep the entire household treasure in one place, to pass it down through the generations. But during the Middle Ages it underwent much more frequent changes than later on. From the beginning, the ecclesiastical treasury of precious relics must have been considerable. As well as these, the treasure vaults contained insignia, a collection of non-religious jewellery and sumptuous tableware made of precious metal. There were also silver and gold, both minted and unminted, and documents. These were primarily deeds establishing ownership to possessions and legal titles to earthly power. The huge collection of holy relics acted as ecclesiastical or 'divine' endorsements and guarantees. In those days a princely treasure represented his movable private fortune, which he could use to display his princely power in public, or bestow as gifts to show his princely generosity. It was also wealth that could be quickly converted into money in times of need.

It appears that in Vienna the treasure and the archives were kept separately from a relatively early date. But it was only later that they were systematically organised. In 1364 a common 'household treasure' was mentioned for the first time. It was to be managed on the principle of seniority and not to be disposed of. This was an idea that the Emperor Rudolf II and the Emperor Matthias also strove to carry on.

However, from 1440 onwards, we hear increasingly often of the treasure being pawned, but also about the new ducal and royal crowns. Frederick III's private imperial crown, which he brought with him to Rome in 1452, must have been particularly splendid. However he was crowned as Emperor with the state sovereign crown, which was sent to him from Nuremberg.

Although Frederick III redeemed the pawned jewels, his son Maximilian I, who had to fight for his Burgundian inheritance and was therefore always in need of money, was often obliged to pawn some of the Burgundian treasure. Its value had once been inestimable, though he had only inherited what was left to his household after the death of Charles the Bold. Some pieces later returned to the Hapsburg treasure, such as Philip the Good's court goblet and the 'Ainkhürn' (Unicorn) Sword.

We have little detailed knowledge about the treasure possessed by the Emperor Ferdinand I. However the assumption appears to be correct that he imported to Vienna principles that had been developed in Italy since the beginning of the

Renaissance. These stressed artistic and aesthetic concerns, as a well as dynastic, for the collection. That is expressed in the often interchangeable usage in Ferdinand's time of the words 'treasure' or 'art' collection for the same possessions.

Two items among Ferdinand I's possessions became of paramount importance in the imperial treasury. These were the great agate bowl and the 'Ainkhürn' Sword. Their cultural value was deemed so important that, after Ferdinand I's death in 1564, his sons declared them to be 'inalienable heirlooms of the house of Austria', which were to be safeguarded by the oldest in the family, following the principle of seniority. Some of these possessions came to the Emperor Rudolf II, who took them with him to Prague, which he had made his residence. Before this he had built a 'treasure gallery' in his Vienna castle.

We know about this Emperor's art collection through the inventory that was made of it, but we do not have information about his treasury, whose most splendid object must have been the imperial household crown, made for him in 1602. The Emperor Rudolf, whose collections were to some extent systematically organised, pursued with his own characteristic stubbornness the idea of a common art and treasure collection for the house of Austria. The Emperor Ferdinand II then took the decisive step in this direction with the so-called establishment of primogeniture in 1621 or 1635, respectively. According to this, all the household jewellery and art treasures – present or future – were to be kept, through the succession of primogeniture, as the 'inalienable property of the ruling house' and no longer connected to the 'country and people'.

Emperor Matthias added the orb and sceptre to Rudolf's imperial household crown. Shortly after Rudolf II's death in 1612, Matthias also began bringing the most precious pieces from the Prague treasure and art collections to Vienna. Thus he prevented them being plundered by the Swedes in 1648.

Detailed descriptions of the imperial treasures were only preserved from the time of the Emperor Leopold I. These help us draw conclusions about Ferdinand II's treasures, which were still accommodated in the treasure gallery. They were kept standing opposite the windows in 13 black-stained cabinets, decorated with gilded eagles crowned with Ferdinand III's monogram. The cabinet doors had precious paintings on them, presumably framed pictures. The exhibition displayed things that belonged together. The thirteenth cabinet contained the most valuable pieces, among which were the following: Rudolf's imperial household crown, together with the orb and sceptre completed under Matthias, a copy of the imperial crown, richly set with diamonds, which had first been worn by Ferdinand III. This cabinet also contained the Bohemian insignia and the crown of Stefan Bocskai. Beside them were other precious treasures, including the extremely valuable 2,680 carat Colombian emerald, which Dionysio Miseroni had carved in 1641 to make a vessel. By the pillars of the window wall, opposite the cabinets, there were tables inlaid with gorgeous marquetry, on which stood cabinets containing small precious items. The last table held an outstandingly valuable object, the late antique, great agate bowl belonging to the 'inalienable heirlooms of the house of Austria'. By that time the keys to the coffins of the Hapsburgs were already kept in the treasury. According to descriptions made in the 17th century, the inventory, bound in red velvet, also lay on one of these tables. It is lost without trace. Its loss is particularly regrettable because the next full inventory was not made until 1750.

Countless busts and other indoor sculptures gave the baroque treasury an expressly dynastic-representative character, in order to impress strongly upon visitors the greatness and importance of the 'ruling house'. The Renaissance art-chamber character was less in evidence.

We know little about the treasury in the time of the Emperor Charles VI. At that time, besides the 'secular treasury', there was a second treasury, the 'small secret treasury', for which we still have the inventory made in 1731. There were many precious jewels, some of which may have been among those that Maria Theresia sold to finance the War of Austrian Succession. In the inventory made in 1750 by her treasurer, Joseph Angelo de France, we note the lack of diamond jewellery. On the other hand we see that in this new treasury set up under Maria Theresia, there are numerous objects which were not named in the 'treasure gallery' of Ferdinand III and Leopold I. For the first time, we find numerous bronze statuettes decoratively arranged on the 13 cabinets and wall shelves. We know of some of these from the art treasure inventories made by Emperors Rudolf II and Matthias. Under the direction of Joseph Angelo de France, the treasury resumed its character as an art collection. There was a shift of emphasis with the creation of a separate jewel chamber. After the death of her consort Franz Stephan of Lorraine in 1765, the Empress displayed his valuable diamond and jewellery collection in this chamber. The collection contained the famous Florentine diamond.

In the reign of Emperor Joseph II, the administration of the ecclesiastical and secular treasury was separated. The former was put under the control of the Court chaplain, together with the relics and paraments (vestments and ornaments) of the individual court chapels. The paintings, of which there were still a considerable number, were gradually added to the imperial picture gallery.

The turmoil of the Napoleonic period brought about important changes for the treasury. In 1794 the treasure belonging to the Order of the Golden Fleece was removed from Brussels to Vienna and deposited, at first provisionally, in the treasury. In 1796 the imperial jewels were removed from Aix-la-Chapelle and Nuremberg to safeguard them from General Jourdan's approaching French troops. They were given into the keeping of the Imperial Commissar Freiherr von Hügel in Regensburg. On the instructions of the Emperor Franz II, they were finally deposited in the Vienna treasury in 1800. In 1804 Franz II established the hereditary Austrian lands as the new hereditary Empire of Austria. He made the imperial private insignia the official insignia of this new empire. Then the treasury came to possess a huge wealth of insignia, unparalleled throughout Europe. With the abolition of the Holy Roman Empire in 1806, its insignia lost their official character. However, they were only appreciated at their true value after they had become mere historical mementos.

This official and historical collection of insignia now dominated the treasury and overwhelmed its character as an art collection, which it had had since the time of Maria Theresia. So it seemed necessary to weed some of the insignia out. From the late 18th century on, antique works of art or works with antique themes had begun to be removed to the imperial coin and antiques cabinet. However, these objects and also treasury items with a 'purely artistic' character were taken out of the imperial coin and antiques cabinet and incorporated into the Ambrasian collection during the Napoleonic period, when the most important pieces of this Ambrasian collection were brought to safety from the Tyrol to Vienna,

At first the most valuable objects made of jewels and precious metals remained in the treasury. Indeed, similar pieces were even added from the Ambrasian collection (to the treasury). Nevertheless, the imperial collections continued to be divided up in the newly adopted way. In 1871 there was a major re-organisation of the collection.

This led to the building of the Kunsthistorisches Museum. All the works of art remaining in the treasury were removed and finally installed in this Kunsthistorisches Museum in 1891. Since then, the secular treasury has only contained objects designed to express, through their cultural or material value, the historic importance and power of the imperial household, or to serve as mementos of individual family members. Significant treasury additions were only made to the private diamond jewellery, in particular, parures (sets of jewellery, ornaments or trimmings) created or reworked for the Empress Elizabeth. However in 1898, the Oath-Cross of Allegiance and the Potence of the Order of the Golden Fleece were still deposited there for safekeeping.

Twenty years later the treasury suffered its heaviest loss through the First World War's unhappy outcome for Austria. In 1918 the Emperor Charles and his family had to leave Austria and took their private jewellery with them into exile. The St Germain Peace Treaty allowed the successor states the right to claim various objects from their cultural heritage. Since then the treasury has become another collection of the Kunsthistorisches Museum. In 1938 on Hitler's orders, the insignia and jewellery of the Holy Roman Empire were brought to Nuremberg and the treasury was closed. The kidnapped objects were returned to Vienna in 1946. Like the other precious objects in the treasury, they survived the Second World War intact.

In 1954 the treasury could at last reopen. This meant that for the first time since that of the Emperor Joseph II, the secular and ecclesiastical treasury were together in one place. This single display of the secular and ecclesiastical treasury reflects the double-natured power and position of the ruler of the Christian West, as it continued until the time of Charles VI. That is why today there is almost nowhere else where the presence of a thousand years of western history can be experienced more intensely than in the Vienna treasury.

The Secular Treasury

The Insignia of the Austrian Hereditary Homage

The beginning and basis of the rule of the house of Austria was the duchy and later archduchy of Austria, with which the Roman King Rudolf of Hapsburg, enfeoffed his sons, Albrecht and Rudolf, after the victorious battle against King Ottokar of Bohemia in 1278. Here, as in the other 'hereditary lands' under Hapsburg rule, the enthroning of a new ruler was not accompanied by his coronation, as happened in the later Hapsburg kingdoms of Hungary and Bohemia, but by a ceremony of homage, in which the estates in the parliament swore obedience to the ruler and he guaranteed to respect their rights. However, at this ceremony sovereign insignia were also used: the Austrian archduke's coronet, an orb and sceptre. The archduke's coronet was kept in the Klosterneuberg Monastery, according to its foundation privilege of 1616, and was only at the disposal of the ruler for the homage ceremony. The estates were represented by the 'hereditary offices' going back to the ancient court offices. They had their own insignia and were hereditary in the country's foremost families.

Orb and Sceptre belonging to the Insignia of the Austrian Hereditary Homage
Prague, 3rd quarter of 14th century.
Silver gilt
Orb: 16 cm high;
Sceptre: 79.6 cm long
(Inv. No. XIV 44, XIV 43)

As the portrait of the Emperor Matthias as King of Bohemia shows (see page 39), both these power-symbols belonged to the insignia of the King of Bohemia until the early 17th century. The picture in the background shows the Austrian archducal coronet, which was made for Joseph II's entry into Frankfurt for his coronation as king in 1764 (see page 40).

**Dog collar, falconer's bag, falcon lure (mock birds)
and two falcon hoods**
Vienna, 1835 (?).
Green and red leather, green velvet embroidered with gold,
silver gilt, feathers;
(Inv. Nos. XIV 40, XIV 36. XIV 39, XIV 37, XIV 38)

The five objects were the insignia of the Hereditary Grand Master
of the Hunt and the Grand Master Falconer at the Hereditary
Homage of the Estates of Lower Austria in 1835 and the Estates of
the Princely County of Tyrol in the year 1838.

The Hereditary Banner of Austria
Austria, 1705.
Silk, gold, silver, wood;
Flag pole 248 cm long
(Inv. No. XIV 34)

The hereditary banner belonged to the archducal insignia of Austria
above and below the Enns. The arms of the two provinces adorn
the two sides of the flag. It was an ancient privilege of the archduke
to have the banner carried in front of him.

The Empire of Austria

The hereditary Austrian empire was established on 11th August 1804, in response to Napoleon's self-proclamation as Emperor of the French and the dissolution of the Holy Roman Empire resulting from his victories. The new Austrian Empire covered all the lands held by the Hapsburgs at that time, that is to say, the Austrian hereditary lands as well as the kingdoms of Hungary and Bohemia. When a new European order was established at the Congress of Vienna after the fall of Napoleon, the Italian provinces which were assigned to Austria united to become the kingdom of Lombardy-Venice. This kingdom then became part of the Austrian Empire. With the Austro-Hungarian settlement in 1867, the lands belonging to the Hungarian crown of St Stephen were again separated from those belonging to the Austrian Empire. This gave rise to the imperial and royal double monarchy of Austria-Hungary, united in the person of the Hapsburg ruler.

In 1804 the crown of the Emperor Rudolf II, the so-called imperial household crown, became the official insignia of the new imperial state. After the establishment of the double monarchy of Austria-Hungary, this crown remained the symbol of the imperial Austrian half, whereas St Stephen's crown, kept in Budapest, became the official insignia of the kingdom of Hungary.

The new Empire also took over the remaining Orders of Merit that had been founded by the Empress Maria Theresia. They continued until the end of the monarchy in 1918.

LEFT

Emperor Franz I of Austria (1768-1835) wearing the Austrian imperial robes.
Friedrich von Amerling (1803-87),
Vienna, 1832.
Oil on canvas;
260 x 164 cm
(Inv. No. GG 8618)

Franz I is wearing Rudolf II's crown and the 1615 sceptre that went with it. He wears the collars – ornamental chains of office – of the four Orders of the House of Austria, whose Grand Master the Emperor was: the Golden Fleece, the Order of St Stephen, the Order of Leopold and the Order of the Iron Crown. The orb lies on the cushion to the left.

Bust of Emperor Rudolf II (1552-1612)
Adriaen de Vries (c. 1545-1626)
Prague, 1607.
Bronze, red-brown patina;
54.5 cm high
(Inv. No. KK 5491)

Rudolf wears the Golden Fleece on a ribbon. On his shoulder-pieces the allegorical figures of Victory and Fame can be seen. The bust is signed and dated on the back of the plinth.

The Crown of Emperor Rudolf II, from 1804 the Crown of the Empire of Austria
Detail: Fleur de lys
Jan Vermeyen (before 1559-1608), Prague, 1602.
Gold, enamel, diamonds, rubies, sapphire, pearls, red velvet;
28.3 cm high
(Inv. No. XIa 1)

In 1424 the Emperor Sigismund allowed the ancient imperial crown to be kept 'for all time' in Nuremberg, from whence it was brought for each coronation. The Emperor also had a private crown, designed as a mitre crown. It consists of the crown circlet with lily wreath, the high imperial top-arch from forehead to neck, and the mitre, which symbolises the high-priestly grace of God. Jan Vermeyen united these three elements in well-proportioned harmony. He then picked them out with precious jewels, each bearing the meaning it had on the ancient imperial crown. The diamonds on the crown circlet symbolise Christ, the guarantor of the King's rule. The number eight represents the Emperor, in whom heaven and earth are joined. With their Pentecostal red, the rubies in the fleur de lys refer to the King's wisdom. The blue sapphire standing over the cross means heaven, the goal of the good king and all believers. The mitre, which was formerly made of material, has no precious stones. The pearls are like lights, which outline all the shapes.

Emperor Rudolf II's Crown. Details: two panels of the mitre.
LEFT: **Rudolf II as Imperator (Commander-in-Chief)**
ABOVE: **His Coronation as King of Hungary in Pressburg, riding over the coronation hill**

The Mitre's four golden panels illustrate Rudolf II's four main titles, which are inscribed on the inside of the crown circlet: 'IMPERATOR (Commander-in-Chief), AVGVSTVS (Emperor), REX HVNGARIAE (King of Hungary), ET BOHEMIAE (and Bohemia)'. The first plate shows him as conqueror and prince of peace. The second shows his coronation as Roman King in Regensburg (1.11.1575), by which he was designated Emperor. The third shows him as King of Hungary (coronation on 26.9.1572) and the fourth as King of Bohemia (coronation on 22.1 1575). The fourfold portrayal of Rudolf, unprecedented on insignia of sovereignty such as a crown, shows his strong sense of his own dignity and also the crown's private character.

RIGHT
The Austrian Orb
ascribed to Andreas Osenbruck
(worked in Prague c. 1610 - after
1625), Prague, between 1612 and
1615.
Gold, enamel, diamonds,
rubies, sapphire, pearls;
26.9 cm high
(Inv. No. XIa 3)

The Emperor Matthias added
the orb and sceptre to Rudolf's
crown. The type of jewels – no
emeralds here either – and the
decoration, had to copy the
style of the crown. The spherical
orb represents the world and
symbolises the Emperors's claim
to universal rule.

The Austrian Sceptre
Andreas Osenbruck
(worked in Prague c. 1610- after 1625), Prague, 1615.
'Unicorn' (narwhal horn), gold, enamel, diamonds, rubies, sapphire, pearls;
75.5 cm long
(Inv. No. XIa 2)

Osenbruck signed and dated the sceptre in the capsule at the top of the staff. On the outside of the capsule there is the monogram of the Emperor Matthias and the year he began to reign, 1612. The choice of precious stones again copies the crown. The mythical unicorn could not be caught by a hunter, but tamely laid his head in a virgin's lap. This was seen as an image of Christ's incarnation. The virgin was Mary. The unicorn's horn became a symbol of Christ, his divine power and mission of redemption. It then became a sign of the worldly ruler legitimated by him. From the 1530s, Matthias' orb and sceptre replaced the insignia of Emperor Ferdinand I, which then went to the Bohemian crown. The old Bohemian insignia from the 14th century went to the archduchy of Austria (see p. 10).

Robes of a Knight of the Austrian Order of the Iron Crown
Design: Philipp von Stubenrauch (1784-1848), Vienna, 1815/16.
Violet velvet, orange velvet, silver embroidery, lace, ostrich feathers, nappa leather;
(Monturdepot, Inv. No. EK III-3)

Circular mantle with wide border, depicting the Theodolinden crown with palm
leaves and laurel branches, oak leaf wreaths with the Order's motto 'AVCTA ET
AVITA (inherited and increased)'. Napoleon founded an Order of the Iron Crown
in 1805. When the provinces of Lombardy-Venice fell to Austria, Emperor Franz I
founded the Austrian version of the Order on 1.1.1816.

**Designs for the Robes
of the Emperor of Austria**
Philipp von Stubenrauch
(1784-1848),
Vienna, 1830.
Water colour on cardboard;
25.3 x 32 cm
(Inv. No. XVI B 41)

Stubenrauch was the costume
manager of the court theatre
in Vienna. The Emperor put a
cross by the design on the left,
which, essentially, was the one
that was made up.

**The Mantle of the
Austrian Emperor**
Design: Philipp von
Stubenrauch (1784-1848)
Execution: Johann Fritz,
Master Gold Embroiderer,
Vienna, 1830.
Red and white velvet,
gold embroidery, sequins,
ermine, white silk;
276 cm long
(Inv. No. XIV 117)

The scatter pattern on
the material consists of
double eagles with the
Austrian arms on the
escutcheon, bordered
by oak and bay leaves.

The Coronation Robes of the Lombard-Venetian Kingdom
Design: Phillipp von Stubenrauch (1784-1848)
Execution: Johann Fritz Master Gold Embroiderer, Vienna, 1838.
Blue and orange velvet, white moiré, gold and silver embroidery, ermine, lace; 269 cm long
(Inv. Nos. XIV 118, XIV 119)

The Lombard-Venetian Kingdom united the Northern Italian provinces which had been ceded to Austria at the Congress of Vienna in 1815. The Emperor Ferdinand I was crowned king in Milan on 6.9.1838. The robes were made for this occasion and their pale border shows the iron crown. In 1859 Austria had to withdraw from Lombardy.

Emperor Ferdinand I of Austria wearing the Lombard-Venetian Coronation Robes
Signed: A Weissenböck, Vienna, about 1838.
Water colour on paper;
60 x 49 cm
(Inv. No. XVI B 43)

The water colour is the only evidence showing how the king wore the tiny Iron Crown with the help of a crown-shaped attachment. It was designed by the painter Peter Fendi, together with the sceptre and orb. All three pieces were broken up and sold in Italy in 1871-72. The Iron Crown is now once again kept at Monza.

The Hapsburg-Lorraine Household Treasure

The Hapsburg-Lorraine household treasure is the family treasure of the house of Austria and thus the basis of the secular treasury. It was part of the family primogeniture *fidei-commissum* of the imperial art collections. Among the treasures are the formerly private imperial coronation insignia, which became the official insignia of Austria in 1804. There is also a large collection of jewels. The agate bowl and the so-called Ainkhürn (Unicorn) are the two 'inalienable heirlooms of the house of Austria'. There are the christening vessels and robes as well as countless mementos of individual members of the 'ruling house'. Among the latter, there are objects of historical interest relating to Napoleon I, Emperor of the French, and his second wife Marie Louise, Archduchess and Imperial Princess of Austria, as well as to their son Napoleon Franz Charles, the King of Rome and later Duke of Reichstadt. Finally, there are personal objects belonging to the unfortunate Emperor Maximilian of Mexico, the younger brother of the Emperor Franz Joseph.

This treasure was originally substantially larger. After 1871 all the art collections of the imperial household were transferred to the Kunsthistorisches Museum, which had been specially built for them. The treasury retained only those items of the household treasure that would document the power and greatness of the imperial household through their symbolic, historical or material nature and value.

Many precious jewelled vessels, cameos, small sculptures made of bronze, ivory and other materials and much of the goldwork, which today add to the fame of the Kunsthistorisches Museum, came from the treasury. Some of them can be traced back to the Emperor Rudolf II's art treasury. Maria Theresia had an inventory made of this 'household treasure' in 1750. This was the treasury's first full inventory that is still preserved.

Inventory of the treasury, commissioned by the Empress Maria Theresia in the year 1750.

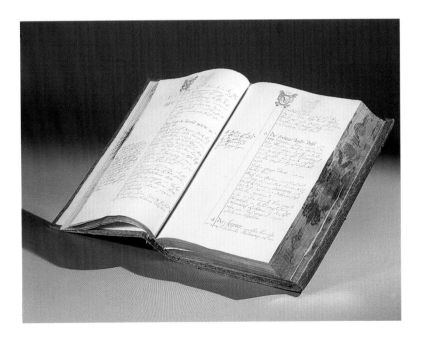

The Emperor Napoleon
Empress Marie Louise
Jean Baptiste Isabey (1767-1855), Paris, 1810.
Gouache on ivory; frame: brass gilt;
Each 24.8 x 16.5 cm, with frame: 31.9 x 24.2 cm
(Inv. No. XIV 148)

Napoleon and Marie Louise are portrayed in the clothes
they wore for their wedding on 2.4.1810. The Empress's
diamond and ruby diadem and necklace were Napoleon's
wedding present to her

The King of Rome's Rocking-Cradle Throne
Design: Pierre Paul Prud'hon (1758-1823), Cast mould: Henri-Victor Rouguier
(1758- after 1830), Execution: Jean-Baptiste-Claude Odiot (1763-1850) and
Pierre-Philippe Thomire (1751-1843), Paris, 1811.
Silver gilt, gold, mother of pearl, velvet, silk, tulle;
216 cm high
(Inv. No. XIV 28)

Gift of the city of Paris to the Empress Marie Louise on the occasion of the birth of
her son Napoleon-Franz-Charles on 20.3.1811. More than 280 kg silver was used in
the workmanship. The heir to the throne received the title King of Rome at his birth
and, after Napoleon's death, the title Duke of Reichstadt. He died in Vienna in 1832.

Empress Marie Louise's Jewellery Casket
Martin Guillaume Biennais (1764-1843) and Augustin Dupré (1748-1833).
Paris, 1810.
Silver gilt, velvet, silk; 28.8 cm high, 54.7 cm long, 34.7 cm wide
(Inv. No. XIV 153)

According to tradition, the casket contained the jewels that Napoleon gave to Marie Louise at their wedding. Napoleon's imperial arms are on the middle of each side of the box. The bas-reliefs on the sides of the lid show the 'Aldobran Wedding', as in the famous antique fresco.

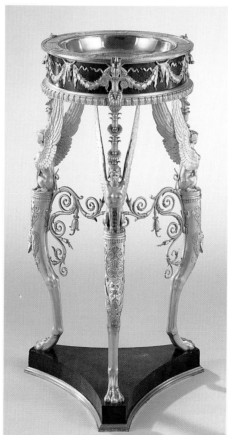

Tripod with Basin
Luigi Manfredini (1771-1840) and Francesco Manfredini, Milan, 1811.
Bronze gilt, silver gilt, lapis lazuli; 81.5 cm high, 37 cm diameter
(Inv. No. XIV 152)

According to tradition, the tripod was a present from the city of Milan to Napoleon and Marie Louise on the occasion of the birth of the heir to the throne in 1811. It is copied from an antique bronze tripod from Pompei, which can be seen today in the Museo Nazionale in Naples

Christening Table Cloth, Two Christening Robes, Christening Candle
Table Cloth: Vienna, 1762; robe on right: Vienna, end of 18th century;
robe on left: Vienna, 1830; candle: Vienna, 1868.
Silver moiré with pattern in satin, gold lace; cambric, gold embroidery,
pillow lace; pink satin, tulle lace; wax painted with coloured oils;
178 x 116, 65 cm long, 72 cm long, 73 cm long
(Inv. Nos. XIV 10 XIV 11, A 208 D 109)

The pink robe, which goes with the tulle cap, was used at the christening of the
Emperor-to-be Franz Joseph (1830) and his brothers and sisters, Maximilian
(of Mexico, 1832), Archduke Charles Ludwig (1833), Archduchess Maria Anna
(1835) and Archduke Ludwig Viktor (1842).

Christening Jug and Basin
RIGHT: **Detail of the Christening Basin**
with the Arms of Carinthia
Spanish Master, 1571.
Gold, part enamelled;
Jug: 34.5 cm high; basin 61.5 cm diameter
(Inv. No. XIV 5, XIV 6)

The set, into which about 10.5 kg gold is worked, was given
as a wedding present in 1571 by the Carinthian estates to the
Archduke Charles of Inner Austria and Maria of Bavaria.
From the 17th century onwards, the precious basin, originally
intended for secular use, was used for baptism.

Christening Jug
Jan Vermeyen (before 1559-1608) Prague, about 1600.
Gold, part enamelled, rubies;
15.5 cm high
(Inv. No. XIV 7)

This elegant masterpiece from the imperial court
workshop was probably made for Archduke Ferdinand
(who later became Emperor Ferdinand II), who had
married Maria Anna of Bavaria in 1600. The first of
her seven children was born in 1601.

Store Cupboard for the Coffin Keys of the Hapsburgs
Alexander Albert, Court Cabinet-maker, Vienna 1895.
Walnut and other wood;
243 cm high, 149 cm wide, 64 cm deep
(Inv. No. XVI A 24)

The cupboard contains the keys to the 139 coffins, which are to be found in the Capuchin crypt in
Vienna, in Seckau, Bozen, Gmünd, Linz, Neuberg and Mantua. In the middle section are the keys to
the coffins of the Emperors and his nearest relations. The side compartments contain the keys to the
coffins of the other members of the house of Austria. The oldest keys date from the 17th century.

The Crown of Stefan Bocskai
Turkish, about 1605.
Gold, rubies, spinels, emeralds, turquoise, pearls, silk;
23.2 cm high, 18.8-22 cm diameter
(Inv. No. XIV 25)

The Calvinistic nobleman Stefan Bocskai (1557-1606) rose against Rudolf II on religious grounds and after great military successes had himself elected as Prince of Siebenbürgen and Hungary. The Turkish Sultan Ahmed recognised him and had him crowned by the Grand Vizier Lala Mehmed Pascha in 1605. The Hungarian parliament had the crown brought to Vienna by the Palatine Georg Thurzo in 1610, where it henceforth remained as a reminder of this brief historical episode.

Diamond Sabre
Turkish, 2nd half of 17th century, diamond-studded
Vienna, about 1712.
Damascus steel (with meteoric iron?), gold, silver gilt,
diamonds, a zircon, wood, leather;
91.5 cm long; sheath 82.5 cm long
(Inv. No. XIa 50)

Inscription on the medallion under the angle: 'In the name of God the All Merciful'; along the back: 'Help from God, speedy victory and good tidings for believers'. The silver gilt ornamentation is Turkish. The sabre was decorated, partly with very old diamonds, for the coronation of Charles VI as King of Hungary in 1712. Maria Theresia also wore it at her Hungarian coronation.

Case for the Crown of Stefan Bocskai
Detail of the cover material
Persian, Isfahan (?), about 1600.
Silk;
(Inv. No. XIV 184)

The design of figures, bordered by flowers, shows a lady reading. A servant offers her a bowl with his right hand and in his left he holds a long-necked bottle. The artist's signature is in the lady's book: 'Mu'min'. The precious material probably came from the court of Shah Abbas the Great (1587-1628) in Isfahan.

The Emerald Vessel
Dionysio Miseroni, Prague, 1641.
2,680 carat emerald, gold enamelled;
10.9 cm high, 8.5 cm long, 7.2 cm wide
(Inv. No. KK2048)

The Emperor Rudolf II acquired this gigantic emerald from the Muzo mine in Colombia. In order to avoid too great loss, the carving follows the unhewn stone, which consists of two crystals that have grown together. This explains its irregular shape. The lid is cut out of the inside of the vessel.

Aquamarine
Setting: Vienna (?), about 1800.
492 carat Russian (?) aquamarine, gold;
5.8 cm high, 7.4 cm long, 4.55 cm wide
(Inv. No. KK 1911)

The translucent stone is displayed standing on its own. It swings on a stand with delicate serpent feet.

Pear-shaped Opal
Setting: South German, about 1600.
Slovak precious opal, gold enamelled.
7.2 cm high
(Inv. No. XIa 52)

Family Tree of the Kings and Emperors of the House of Hapsburg
Tree: Vienna, about 1725/30.
Intaglios: Christoph Dorsch (1676-1732), Nuremberg.
Gold, chalcedony;
29.2 cm high 17.4 cm wide
(Inv. No. KK XII 783)

The rhomboid crown of the tree contains the pictures of Rudolf I (1218/1273-1291) up to Charles VI (1685/1711-1740).

Golden Rose
Giuseppe Spagna (1765-1839) and
Pietro Paolo Spagna (1793-1861),
Rome, 1818/19.
Gold; base-plate: verde antico;
about 60 cm high without the
base-plate
(Inv. No. XIV 19)

On the fourth Sunday in Lent
(Laetare Sunday) the pope always
blessed a golden rose, in order to
give it to a deserving institution
or person. In 1819 Pope Pius VII
dedicated this rose to Carolina
Augusta, the fourth wife of the
emperor Franz I of Austria.
Twelve roses symbolise the twelve
apostles, the thirteenth on the top,
which contains musk and balsam,
represents Christ.

The 'La Bella Hyacinth'
Setting: Vienna, 1687.
416 carat garnet or almandine, gold, silver gilt, enamel;
19.9 x 15.8 cm, stone; 6.8 cm high
(Inv. No. XIa 51)

The internal setting with white branches is probably
French work from the early 15th century. However,
the stone is not mentioned until the inventory of 1619.
Even then it was called the 'La Bella Hyacinth', even
though it is not a hyacinth. After it had been lost to the
imperial treasure, Leopold I bought it back in 1687.
The new setting shows the high value that was placed
on the stone: the imperial double eagle, with sword and
sceptre, holding the arms of Hungary and Bohemia in
its claws.

**Grand Cross and Cross of the Military
Order of Maria Theresia, together
with the Star and Cross of the
Hungarian Order of St Stephen**
Vienna, 1765 and 1757; Vienna, 1st half
of 19th century.
Gold, silver, diamonds, emeralds, rubies;
10.6 cm high, 6 cm high, 10.4 cm
diameter, 8.3 cm high
(Inv. Nos. XIa 16, XIa 17, XIa 20, XIa 21)

Both Orders were founded by Maria
Theresia. She established the Military
Order named after herself on the
occasion of the Austrian victory over the
Prussians at Kolin on 18.6.1757. She
established the Order of St Stephen in
1764 on the occasion of the appointment
of her son Joseph II as Roman King. The
order named after the Hungarian King St
Stephen was the monarchy's highest civil
Order of Merit.

Hungarian Opal Belt
Egger brothers, Budapest, 1881.
Gold enamelled, Slovakian opals,
diamonds, rubies;
(Inv. No. XIb 41)

The belt belongs to a parure (set of
ornaments). This was a gift from the
city of Budapest to Princess Stéphanie
of Belgium on her betrothal to Crown
Prince Rudolf in 1881. It consists of
belt, necklace, ear rings, ten bodice-
clasps, two sleeve clasps and five hair
pins. The design was modelled on
ornaments worn by 16th-century
Hungarian magnates.

The Agate Bowl
Constantinople (?), 4th century.
Agate;
76 cm wide including the handles
(Inv. No. XIV 1)

The bowl was cut out of a single piece of agate, probably at the court of Constantine. For centuries it has been regarded as the 'greatest masterpiece' in the whole treasury. By a deed of 1564, Maximilan II and his brothers declared it to be an 'inalienable heirloom of the house of Austria'. They valued it so highly, not mainly because it was a masterpiece of antique precious stone carving, but because, through a natural miracle, it bore a mysterious inscription. In a certain light, the name of Christ (XRISTO) appears inscribed at the bottom of the bowl in the grain of the stone. This is probably why the idea arose that the bowl was the Holy Grail.

**Empress Maria Theresia
(1717-1780)**
Matthäus Donner (1704-56), Vienna, 1750.
Bronze with brown patina, marble;
68 cm high
(Inv. No. KK 6142)

The bust was installed in a wall-niche in the
'Cabinet of Coins and Medals' of the imperial
treasury in 1750. The inscription on the base
celebrates Maria Theresia as Juno Moneta,
'because she restored the ancient world to its
place of honour'. Hence the antique-type
costume. Maria Theresia had the treasury
re-organised

**Emperor Franz Stephen I of Lorraine (1708-
1756)**
Matthäus Donner (1704-56), Vienna, 1750.
Bronze with brown patina, marble;
69 cm high
(Inv. No. KK 6143)

Companion piece to the bust of Maria Theresia,
which also stood in a niche in the Cabinet of
Coins and Medals. The inscription honours Franz
Stephen as Apollo Monetarius because he had
increased the coin treasure. Both busts are
signed and dated on the left hand side. The
casting moulds in lead are to be found in the
collection of the National Mint in Vienna.

The Holy Roman Empire

The insignia and jewels of the Holy Roman Empire can be considered one of the greatest monuments of European history. They are the symbol of an idea of government that began with the coronation of Charlemagne on Christmas Eve in the year 800 and lasted until 1806, when the Emperor Franz II dissolved the Empire under pressure from Napoleon's superior force. At least for medieval people, the Holy Roman Empire was the continuation of the *Imperium Romanum* under the rule of Christ. This explains why the secular insignia are weighted with ecclesiastical and theological significance and why there are so many important relics among the jewels. The latter acted as divine guarantees for rightful rule on earth. Christ had inaugurated it by his sacrifice on the cross and the Holy Roman Emperor was now his representative.

Two particularly significant relics were the great Particle of the Cross and the Holy Lance, in which, according to tradition, a nail from Christ's cross had been incorporated. The latter was probably given by Pope Hadrian to Charlemagne in the year 774. The gift was an allusion to Constantine the Great and the passing on of this power-symbol created a link between the *Imperium Romanum* and the later Holy Roman Empire. That gift and the coronation that followed in the year 800 caused Charlemagne, as the first western Emperor, always to be honoured especially highly. Three jewels, which according to legend were from his grave, were regarded as relics of Charlemagne. Their presence at subsequent coronations was used as a visible token of a legitimate and direct tradition handed down from the first western Emperor to the Emperor being crowned. The new Emperor swore his Coronation Oath on the Carolingian Imperial Evangeliar (Gospel), handwritten in gold on crimson. St Stephen's Purse, a 9th-century reliquary probably made in Rheims containing earth soaked with the blood of the first martyr Stephen, was sunk into the seat of the throne. At his coronation the Emperor was girded with the 'sabre of Charlemagne', an Eastern European work from the early 10th century.

The central item of the insignia was, however, the Crown. It was probably made either for the

The Emperor Charlemagne
Copy after Albrecht Dürer's ideal portrait in Nuremberg, Nuremberg, about 1600.
Oil on canvas;
209 x 119.5 cm
(Inv. No. GG 2771)

Charlemagne was regarded as the founder of the Holy Roman Empire and, anachronistically, he appears in the full regalia. The insignia and robes, whose originals Dürer was able to study for his painting, were mistakenly traced back to Charlemagne.

Emperor Otto the Great or for his son the Emperor Otto II, in the second half of the 10th century, perhaps in the artistically dominant workshops of the Benedictine abbey of Reichenau in the region of Lake Constance, or in Milan. Through a complex theological agenda the crown also symbolises the transcendental character of the medieval concept of world government. The heavenly Jerusalem was imagined as having eight corners. The twelve great jewels on the forehead-plate represent the twelve apostles, corresponding to the twelve tribes of Israel in the Old Testament. The four enamel plates relate to the coronation liturgy in their iconography. The circlet derives from the crowns of the Byzantine Eastern Roman Empire, with whom there was close contact in Otto's time. The top-arch alludes to the top-arches, stuck with feathers, of the Roman Emperor's helmet. From these cross-references, a unique, characteristically shape of crown arose, which was clearly distinct from any other western crown.

The coronation robes that go with the imperial crown jewels are also unique. Apart from the Eagle Dalmatic and the Stole, some of the coronation robes are those made, mainly by Arabic artists in the 12th and 13th centuries, for the Norman kings of Sicily. They were inherited by Frederick II of Hohenstaufen, who then made them part of the imperial treasure.

Apart from the three special items which were kept in the cathedral at Aix-la-Chapelle, the insignia and jewels of the Holy Roman Empire were at the immediate disposal of the Emperor and kept by him in the strongholds of his dominion. In 1424, the Emperor Sigismund was the first to break with this tradition and placed the imperial treasure in the care of the free city of Nuremberg, in order to protect it from the Hussites. With the conquests of Napoleon, the imperial jewels were removed to safety away from the advancing French troops in 1796. On the orders of Franz II, the last Holy Roman Emperor, they were safeguarded in the imperial treasury in Vienna. They remained there until Hitler had them transported to Nuremberg in 1938. After the end of the Second World War they were given back to Austria, whose ancient dynasty had run to 20 Roman Kings and Emperors.

The Robes of the Royal Bohemian Electoral Prince
Vienna or Prague, before the middle of the 17th century.
Material: Italian, 2nd quarter of 17th century.
Silk, gold, ermine;
131 cm high, diameter 270 cm
(Inv. No. XIV 122)

In the background, painting by Hans von Aachen (1522-1615) and his workshop: Emperor Matthias (1557-1619) as King of Bohemia, full length.

**The Coronation Train of Joseph (II)
on the Römerberg in Frankfurt in 1764, detail**
Workshop of Martin van Meytens the Younger
(Johann Dallinger of Dalling, 1741-1806, and others),
Vienna.
Oil on canvas;
358 x 412 cm
(Inv. No. GG 7466)

The painting belongs to a series of six large pictures,
which were originally in Schönbrunn Castle. The detail
shows the two rulers under the baldachin, carried by the
councillors of Frankfurt. The Emperor Franz I Stephen
of Lorraine rides in front, wearing copies of the ancient
coronation robes, and the crown of Rudolf II on his
head. Behind him rides his son Joseph in archducal
robes and his own archducal coronet, which has been
made especially for this occasion. The ancient insignia
were carried in the train by representatives of the
hereditary offices. This coronation on 3.4.1764 was,
famously, recorded for posterity by Johann Wolfgang
von Goethe, who watched it from the Römer (the
Frankfurt Town Hall) and described it in *Dichtung und
Wahrheit* (Part 1, Book 5)

RIGHT

**The Coronation of Joseph II as Roman King
in the Church of St Bartholomew in
Frankfurt on Main, detail**
Workshop of Martin van Meytens the Younger
(Johann Dallinger of Dalling, 1741-1806, and
others), Vienna.
Oil on canvas;
362 x 295 cm
(Inv. No. GG 7468)

The Archbishop of Mainz, accompanied by the
Archbishops of Cologne and Trier, crowns Joseph
II with the imperial crown. The ambassadors of
the secular electoral princes stand behind Joseph.

The Coronation Mantle
Royal court workshop, Palermo, 1133/34.
Silk, gold, pearls, cloisonné enamel, rubies,
spinels, sapphires, garnets, glass;
345 cm wide, 146 cm high
(Inv. No. XIII 14)

As the Cufic inscription on the semi-circular hem tells us, the Mantle was created at the court of King Roger II (1097/1130-1154) in Palermo in the year 528 (according to the Hegira: the Mohammedan era), that is, 1133 or 1134. The Islamic artists decorated the red samite with ancient power-symbols in gold embroidery, bordered with double rows of pearls. In the middle stands the tree of life, and on either side there is a mighty golden lion triumphing over a camel. The straight hem is decorated with 30 little cloisonné enamel compartments and magnificent pearl embroidery. Above the head of each lion there is a round cloisonné enamel plate in quatrefoil. The rosettes on the lions' heads and paws could signify stars. This would be in the tradition of clothing the ruler in a heavenly mantle.

In 1194 the Mantle, with Alb and blue Tunicella passed to the Hohenstaufens by inheritance, as part of the treasure of the Norman Kings. After his coronation in Rome in the year 1220, King Frederick II must have added the robes to the state treasury. Together with the other insignia, they were mentioned, for the first time in Germany in 1246, in the inventory made for their handing over to King Konrad IV at Trifel Castle in the Rhine Palatinate. The adoption of the robes from a foreign past and especially the Coronation Mantle with its striking motifs from a foreign culture are symbolic of the supra-national character of the Holy Roman Empire.

The Blue Tunicella (Dalmatic)
Detail: Cuff
Palermo, Royal Court Workshop, 1st half of 12th century.
Samite, gold embroidery, cloisonné enamel, gold filigree, pearls;
141.5 cm long, 171.5 cm wide at the hem
(Inv. No. XIII 6)

The similarity of the gold embroidery to that on the coronation mantle allows us to assume that it was created at about the same time. The colour of the blue samite was not achieved with purple, as was previously assumed, but with indigo. The palmettes on the cuffs, formed from rows of pearls, are stitched with small threaded gold reeds, a technique that was previously nowhere else to be found. The cloisonné enamel on the hem is stylistically very close to that on the Coronation Mantle.

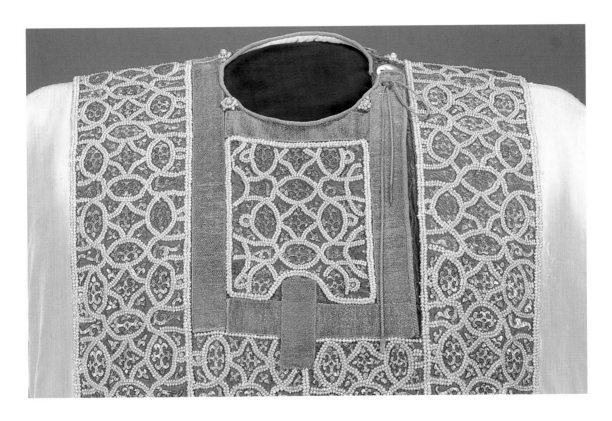

The Alb
Detail: Breast ornamentation
Palermo, Royal Court Workshop, 1181
with later additions.
Silk, gold embroidery, pearls, emeralds,
sapphires, amethyst, spinel, garnet, opal;
154 cm high, 127 cm wide at the hem
(Inv. No. XIII 7)

There are Latin and Arabic inscriptions on
the edge of the broad hem at the bottom.
These tell us that the robe was created in
Palermo under King William II (1153/1166-
1189) in the year 1181. The magnificent
breast ornamentation, which overlays a
previous design, was probably added by the
Emperor Frederick II. Unlike the liturgical
alb, the Alb was originally a royal outer
garment.

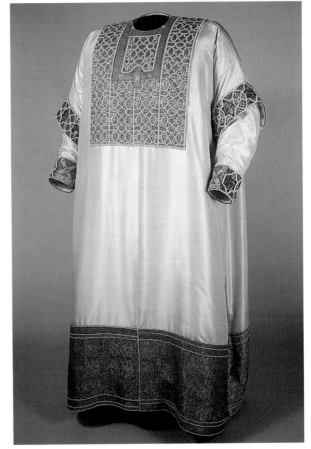

Gloves

Palermo, before 1220.
Red velvet, gold embroidery,
gold appliqué with cloisonné
enamel, pearls, rubies,
sapphires, amethysts, garnets,
spinels, corundums;
26.3 or 27.7 cm long
12 cm wide at the opening

The Hohenstaufen eagle is
on the palm. The gloves were
probably commissioned by
Frederick II for his coronation
in Rome in 1220.

Shoes

German, 1st quarter of
17th century.
Tablet weave: Palermo
12/13th century.
Red samite, tablet weave with
gold thread, pearls, amethysts,
sapphires, emerald, ancient
axinite;
Sole: cow leather;
10.8 cm high,
Soles: 25.8 or 25.6 cm long
(Inv. No. XIII 13)

The cut is 17th century. The
striking decoration is probably
a variant of older shoes from
Sicily.

The Eagle Dalmatic
Detail: Half Figure of a King
South German, about 1330/40,
Material: Chinese, about 1300.
Red silk damask twill, embroidery in
silk and gold, small axinites;
front 165 cm; behind: 160 cm long
138 cm wide at the hem
(Inv. No. XIII 15)

The pattern of the material shows the
Chinese continuous ring of clouds. The
68 eagle medallions are sewn on. The
neck border is decorated with the busts
of six rulers. The other borders have 34
quatrefoil medallions with half or three-
quarter figures of kings and emperors,
who have still not been identified. Like
the Stole made at the same time, the
Eagle Dalmatic, which is first mentioned
in a handing-over deed of 1350, may
have been made for Ludwig of Bavaria
(reigned 1314-1347). It is uncertain
whether it was used at coronations.
However, in a drawing of 1510, Albrecht
Dürer showed Charlemagne wearing
the Eagle Dalmatic, Stole and Imperial
Mantle

Imperial Crown. Forehead-Cross, reverse side

The cross over the forehead-plate is from the time of Henry II (reigned 1002-24). The outer side is shaped as a jewelled cross and symbol of victory. The reverse side shows the bleeding redeemer on the cross, who is at the same time conqueror of death. The imperial crown has a christological agenda. The Emperor reigns as Christ's representative, from whom he derives his power and to whom he has to answer for his deeds. 'By me kings reign' is written on the enamel plate with Christ enthroned.

The Imperial Crown
Detail: Enamel plate with King David

The banderol bears the psalm verse: 'Honor regis iudicium diligit [The king's honour loves righteousness].' David becomes the image of the righteous king. The enamel plates illustrate the most important virtues of the ruler. The artist from the Otto period was under Byzantine influence.

The Imperial Crown
West German or Milan, 2nd half of 10th century, the Crown Cross is early 11th century,
top-arch from the time of Konrad II (1024-39), red velvet cap 18th century.
Gold, cloisonné enamel, precious stones, pearls;
Forehead-plate 14.9 cm high, 11.2 cm wide
(Inv. No. XIII 1)

The basic octagon shape contains the number representing the Emperor. This number 8 appears in many imperial works (for example the Palatine chapel in Aix-la-Chapelle). The four main plates are thickly encrusted with precious stones. The twelve precious stones on the forehead-plate symbolise the twelve apostles, the New Covenant. The twelve stones on the neck plate represent the twelve tribes of Israel, the Old Covenant. The Otto kings saw themselves as the successors of the apostles and of the high priest. The four enamel plates show Christ with two seraphim, King David, King Solomon and King Hezekiah with the prophet Isaiah. The inscriptions explain their connection with the King; they refer to God's grace, righteousness, wisdom and long life. The imperial top-arch from forehead to neck bears the name of Konrad II, set in pearls. The occasion for the making of the crown is said to have been the coronation of Otto the Great in 962 or his son Otto II as co-emperor in 967.

LEFT

The Imperial Orb
Cologne (?), about 1200.
Gold, precious stones, pearls;
21 cm high
(Inv. No. XIII 2)

The Hohenstaufen orb is in
a long tradition descending
from antiquity. The ball
represents the world and
hence world government.
Since the victory of
Christendom, the cross on
top refers to Christ as
Kosmokrator [ruler of the
cosmos]. The Emperor
reigns as his representative.

The Holy Lance
Carolingian, 8th century.
Steel, iron, brass, silver, gold, leather;
50.7 cm long
(Inv. No. XIII 19)

The Carolingian lance is chiselled out in
the middle to insert an iron pin, which has
three knot-like lumps in it. Three brass
crosses are set into the knots. These
probably originally relate to forged-in
particles of a nail from Christ on the cross.
In the 11th century the iron pin was
regarded as a nail from the cross. The lance
itself was thought to have belonged to St
Mauritius (the Empire's patron saint).
During the 13th century, it became the
Holy Lance, with which Longinus pierced
Christ's side. The golden overlaid cuff,
dating from the time of Charles IV (reigned
1346-78), covers a break in the lance's
blade. Its inscription reads: 'Lance and
Nail of the Lord'. The lance was supposedly
given to Charlemagne by Pope Hadrian I.
Under the Otto dynasty, the lance became
a symbol of sovereign rule and might. The
miraculous power of invincibility was ascribed
to it. As the foremost of the imperial
insignia, it ranked above the Crown. Its
power was regarded as the reason for Otto
I's victory over the Hungarians in 955
(Battle of Lechfeld) and over the Slavs. It
was kept in the horizontal arm of the
Imperial Cross.

**Reliquary containing Particle
of the Cross with Case**
Setting: Prague (?), after 1350.
Pine wood, gold;
31.3 cm high, 20.2 cm wide
Leather case: Nuremberg, 1517
(Inv. No. XIII 20 and XIII 35)

It was believed that the large chip of
wood had a nail-hole soaked in Christ's
blood, and it was therefore regarded as
particularly sacred. In this relic of his
passion Christ himself protects the
rulers. It was kept in the shaft of the
Imperial Cross, until Charles the IV
had the gold setting made in the shape
of a processional cross, whose side
arms are painted black.

The Imperial Cross
Detail: the middle part
West German, about 1024-25.
Foot of the cross: Prague 1352.
Oak core, covered with red
material, gold, precious stones,
pearls, niello;
Foot of the cross: silver gilt,
enamel;
95.2 cm high, 70.8 cm wide
(Inv. No. XIII 21)

The Imperial Cross was
originally the reliquary for the
imperial relics. In hollows in
the wooden core lay the Holy
Lance (in the horizontal arm)
and the particle of the cross (in
the shaft). The Cross, richly
decorated with precious stones,
is a symbol of triumph and
victory. The monumental
inscription on its sides explains
its significance: 'Before this
cross of the Lord may the
followers of the evil enemy
flee; and therefore may all
opponents retreat also from
before you Konrad [Konrad I.
1024-39].' The jewels are
bordered in pearl filigree and
bevelled to look like little
cupolas.

The Imperial Sword (Mauritius Sword)
Detail: Sheath panel
Sheath: German, 2nd third of 11th century,
Byzantine or Byzantine-like enamel,
olive wood plated with gold, enamel, garnets;
Sword: German, between 1198 and 1218.
Steel blade with knob and crossbar lightly gilded.
Handle wrapped in silver wire;
110 cm long
(Inv. No. XIII 17)

On the knob are the imperial eagle and the arms of
King Otto IV (1198-1218). The inscription reads:
'BENEDICTUS DO[MINU]S DE[U]S QUI
DOCET MANUS: 'Blessed be the Lord God who
teaches the hand to lead.' That on the crossbar reads:
'CHRISTUS VINCIT CHRISTUS REGNAT
CHRIST[US] INPERAT' (sic): Christ conquers,
Christ reigns, Christ rules.' Figures of rulers, each
with an orb and sceptre in his hands, are worked into
the gold on the sheath. They stand upright if the
Sword is carried with its point upwards. They
represent the 14 kings and emperors, who reigned
from Charlemagne up to and including Henry III
(1039-1056), from whom the sheath originates.

**The Imperial Evangeliar or
Coronation Evangeliar (Gospel)**
Codex: Court of Charlemagne, just
before 800.
236 crimson-dyed parchment pages
gold and silver ink, paints;
32.4 x 24.9 cm
Cover: Hans von Reutlingen, Aix-la-
Chapelle, about 1500.
Silver gilt, precious stones;
34.5 x 24.9 cm
(Inv. No. XIII 18)

The manuscript is the most important of
a small group of manuscripts that were
produced at the court of Charlemagne
after 794, when he had settled in Aix-la-
Chapelle. At his coronation the new king
swore the Oath on this Gospel. His oath
fingers touched the page with the beginning
of the Gospel of John on it. On the front
cover God the Father sits enthroned in
the centre. On either side of him stand
Mary and the Angel of the Annunciation.
In the corners there are medallions with
the symbols of the four evangelists.

**Coronation Evangeliar,
Detail: John the Evangelist**

The Gospel's illustrations consist of
16 canon plates and four pictures of
the evangelists. The pictures are
markedly 'antique' in style. That of
John gives the strongest impression
of spatial depth. The Evangelist's
footstool goes over the frame. There
is a shaft of light in the sky. The
artist came from the East, perhaps
from Constantinople and mysteriously
he still worked in the artistic idiom of
the post-Justinian period around 600.

The 'Sabre of Charlemagne the Great'

Eastern Europe (Hungary?),
1st half of 10th century.
Sabre: Steel blade with partly gilded copper
inlays, wooden handle, fish skin, gold,
silver gilt, precious stones;
Sheath: wood, leather, gold;
90.5 cm long
(Inv. No. XIII 5)

We do not know where the sabre came from or
when it came to belong to the imperial insignia is
unclear. The legends that it is 'Attila's sword' or
'part of the Awar booty of 796' or 'a present from
Harun to Rashid' are completely unfounded.
After the sabre came to be regarded as a relic of
Charlemagne, the new sovereign was girded with
it at his coronation.

St Stephen's Purse

Carolingian, 1st third of 9th century.
Clasp: 15th century, reverse side: about 1827.
Gold plate on wood, precious stones, pearls, glass
Reverse side: silver gilt;
32 cm high
(Inv. No. XIII 26)

The reliquary in the form of a 'purse' (pilgrim's
bag) was said to contain blood-soaked earth from
the martyrdom of St Stephen.

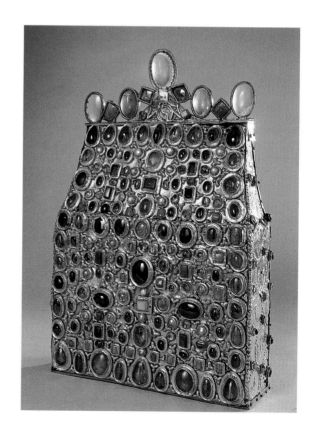

The Coronation of Joseph II as Roman King in Frankfurt in 1764. The dubbing of knights after the Coronation in Frankfurt Cathedral, detail
Atelier of Martin van Meytens the Younger
(Johann Dallinger of Dalling, 1741-1806) and others, Vienna.
Oil on canvas;
363 x 112 cm
(Inv. No. GG 7470)

The dubbing of knights was the first official duty of the new king. Some of the candidates were chosen by the King and some by the Electoral Princes. The list of candidates is being read out by Lieutenant Field Marshal Count Hamilton, Captain of the Royal Household Guard.

The Ceremonial Sword
Palermo, before 1220.
Knob: Prague, 3rd quarter of 14th century
Sword: steel blade; handle and crossbar: wood, gold enamel; knob: silver gilt;
Sheath: wood covered with parchment, lined with linen, gold, enamel, rubies, pearls;
108.5 cm long
(Inv. No. XIII 16)

The sword was among the vestments which Frederick II took to Rome for his coronation as Emperor in 1220. From the 15th century onwards, the crowned Roman King dubbed knights with it. Hence its name. From 1424 on, the Nuremberg envoys brought the imperial insignia to the coronation. They were always knighted.

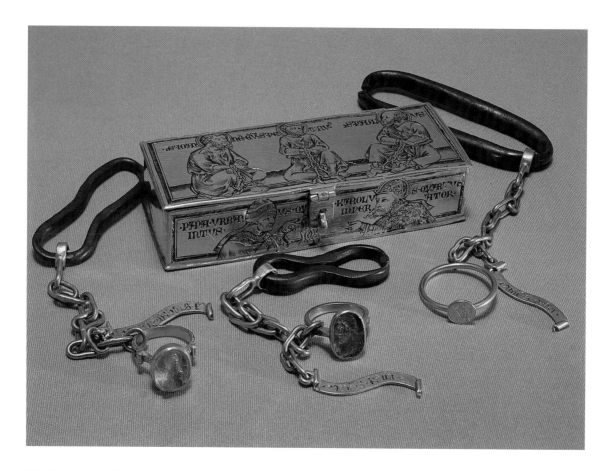

The Reliquary with the Chain Links

Italian engraver, Rome or Prague, about 1368.
Gold, engraved and black-filled enamel, gem stones, iron;
12.5 x 5.1 x 2.8 cm
(Inv. No. XIII 29)

All three chain links, which are from the prison chains of
Saints Peter, Paul and John the Evangelist, are named on
inscribed plates and gold rings. Pope Urban V gave the
relics to the Emperor Charles IV in 1368, as is depicted
on the front of the box. The lid shows the three saints.

The Case for the Imperial Crown

Prague, after 1350.
Leather, iron trimmings;
25 cm high, 30.8 cm diameter
(Inv. No. XIII 30)

The case, sewn in layers, is decorated with blind stamping
and tooled leather, coloured to bring out the design. The
imperial eagle and the Bohemian lion on the lid refer to
Charles IV, who commissioned it. A belt could be passed
through the side-loops to carry the case.

**Two Reliquaries with a Piece
of the Tablecloth from the
Last Supper and a Piece
of Christ's Apron**
Hans Krug the Younger (?)
Nuremberg, 1518.
Silver gilt, precious stones, pearls;
55.9 cm high
(Inv. Nos. XIII 22, XIII 23)

The Last Supper and the Washing
of Feet are engraved on the back,
to explain the reliquaries.

**Reliquary with the Chip of
Wood from Christ's Crib**
Rome or Prague, after 1368.
Gold, precious stones, pearls;
49 x 4.1 x 3.9 cm
(Inv. No. XIII 24)

Pope Urban V gave the reliquary
to the Emperor Charles IV in
1368. The little window in the
middle gives a sight of the wood.

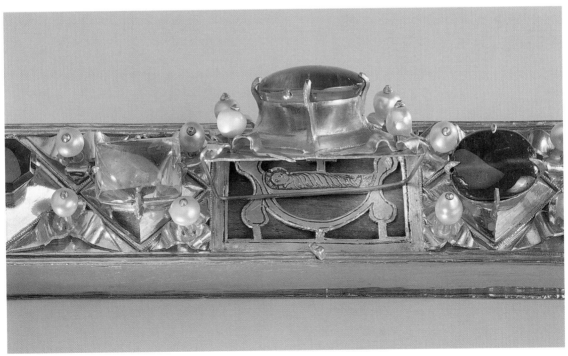

The Burgundian Inheritance and the Order of Golden Fleece

Through the marriage of the Duchess Mary of Burgundy to the Archduke Maximilian of Austria in 1477, the house of Hapsburg acquired some of the richest lands in Europe. Mary's father, Charles the Bold, the last Duke of Burgundy from the house of Valois, fell in battle at Nancy in 1477. The lands he ruled were partly under the French crown and partly belonged to the Holy Roman Empire. France immediately claimed back its fief. However, the lands which were the fief of the Holy Roman Empire not only reverted to the Empire but were also acquired through inheritance by the house of Hapsburg. The legacy included the Netherlands, which were in full bloom, both culturally and economically. This enormous increase of power ensured the dynasty's political rise. In the next generation, by way of inheritance, they added Spain and then Hungary and Bohemia to their Empire.

With this great territorial increase Maximilian and his son, Philip the Fair, also inherited a rich collection of treasures and works of art. This was the remainder of the fabulously valuable Burgundian treasure, the greater part of which had fallen into the hands of the victorious Swiss after the death of Duke Charles the Bold. The Emperor Maximilian was chronically short of money and had to pawn numerous items of this treasure. However what remains in the treasury today still gives us a good impression of the once inestimable wealth of the Dukes of Burgundy.

Finally, the Hapsburgs inherited the Order of the Golden Fleece. This Order had been founded by Duke Philip the Good of Burgundy in 1430, on the occasion of his wedding to Isabella of Portugal, his third wife. The Order had both a political and a religious aim. By bestowing the Order, the Prince wanted to attach the great and powerful men in his lands more closely to himself. Moreover, the Knights of the Order were to defend the Christian faith, for at that time the Turks were already beginning to threaten the Christian West. This was why Philip the Good also seriously contemplated crusades. The Order's emblem, the Golden Fleece, which was borrowed both from the ancient Greek myth of Jason and the Old Testament story of the prophet Gideon, clearly alludes to crusading.

The sovereign of the Order was the Duke, and when the Burgundian inheritance fell to the Hapsburgs, the current head of the Hapsburg family. The wealth, splendour and standing of the Dukes of Burgundy helped make the Golden Fleece rapidly overshadow all the other Orders. It was able to claim the highest rank among the Christian Orders of Knighthood. Hapsburg power then ensured it kept this place. This helps explain why it is one of the few great medieval Orders of Knighthood that are still in existence today.

The number of members was at first limited to 31. In 1516 with the Pope's agreement, the Emperor Charles V raised the number to 51 and later to 60, then 70. This enlargement and the increasing internationality of the knights also shows the continual growth of the Hapsburg Empire.

With the hegemony of the Bourbons in Spain after the War of Spanish succession, they also founded an Order of the Golden Fleece. However, unlike the Hapsburg Order, the Spanish Golden Fleece did not keep the Order's ancient statutes.

Emperor Maximilian I (1449-1519)
Bernhard Strigel (1460-1528), about 1500.
Oil on wood;
60.5 x 41 cm
(Inv. No. GG 922)

This picture is the oldest exemplar of the many
settings and replicas of this portrait by Strigel,
that was clearly regarded as genuine.

Mary of Burgundy (1458-82)
Ascribed to Nicholas Reiser,
Schwaz in Tyrol, about 1500.
Oil on wood;
79 x 46 cm
(Inv. No. GG 4402)

Mary, daughter of Duke Charles the Bold of
Burgundy, was the first wife of the Emperor
Maximilian I. As the heiress of Burgundy, she
brought the territories of the Netherlands to
the house of Austria.

The Tabards for the Heralds of the Duchies of Brabant and Burgundy and the County of Flanders (left to right)

Brussels, 1715, Burgundy, 17th century.
Velvet, gold lamé, silver lamé (for Burgundy);
84 cm long, 129 cm wide; 85.5 cm long,
130 cm wide; 83 cm long, 126 cm wide
(Inv. Nos. XIV 79, XIV 75, XIV 87)

The Throne-of-Grace Trinity
Burgundian-Netherlands, about 1453-67.
Ivory;
14.6 x 11.1 cm
(Inv. No. KK 10.078)

Fire-iron and fire-stone (above left) and the heraldically symmetrical lower-case double 'e' (above right) are the emblems of Duke Philip the Good of Burgundy (1396-1467). In this type of representation of the Trinity, God the Father holds his crucified Son in front of him. The Holy Ghost sits on the horizontal arm of the cross in the shape of a dove. The cross rests on the globe (universe). The baldachin stands for heaven. The archangels Gabriel (with the lily of mercy) and Michael (with the sword of justice) stand on either side of the throne.

**The Burgundian Court Goblet
Detail of the lid**
Burgundian-Netherlands, between
1453 and 1467.
Rock crystal, gold enamel, diamonds,
rubies, pearls
46 cm high
(Inv. No. KK 27)

This masterpiece of late medieval
hardstone carving and goldwork bears
the emblems of Duke Philip the Good
of Burgundy (1396-1467) on its foot-
stand, on the edge of the lid and also
on the lip. The Duke had had these
emblems since 1453. The house of
Valois heraldic fleur de lys, formed
from five diamonds, also appear twice.

**The Collar (ornamental chain) of the
Order of the Golden Fleece**
Flemish, middle of the 15th century.
Gold;
Weight: 507.96 g
(Inv. No. XIV 263)

This Collar, which dates from the foundation of the
Order, is unique, because it consists of 16 separately
carved linked units. This expressed the idea that the
Order's members should hold together in brotherliness.

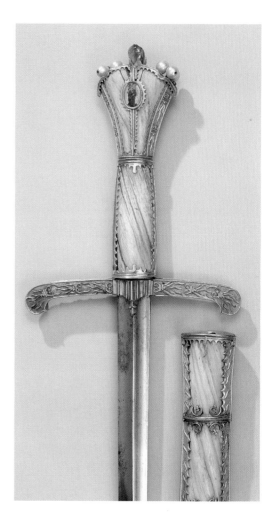

Brooch
Burgundian-Netherlands, about 1430-40
Gold, enamel, diamond, ruby, pearls;
about 5 cm diameter
(Inv. No. KK 130)

The famous brooch shows a fashionably dressed
young couple in a garden of love. The tree-top
over the bride and groom has broken away. The
refined technique of covering little golden figures
wholly with enamel (*émail en ronde bosse*) was
discovered by French court art in about 1400.

The 'Ainkhürn' (Unicorn) Sword
Burgundian-Netherlands, 2nd third of the 15th
century.
Steel, 'unicorn' (narwhal tooth or horn), gold, enamel;
Additions: silver gilt, ruby, pearls;
106 cm long
(Inv. No. XIV 3)

The Sword (with four-edged blade) was especially
highly prized, because its handle and sheath were made
of horn from the legendary miraculous unicorn. It can
be traced back on good authority to Duke Philip the
Good of Burgundy.

The Cross of Allegiance of the Order of the Golden Fleece
French, around 1400 (?).
Stand (a firmly mounted continuation of the Cross) and foot: Flemish, between 1453 and 1467.
Gold, sapphires, rubies, pearls; 36 cm high
(Dep. Prot. 1)

The Cross comes from the possessions of Jean de France, the Duke of Berry. It contained a particle of the true cross at its crossing-point. After 1453, Philip the Good had the foot renewed. It bears his arms and his emblems. The newly created knights and officers of the Order swore their oath on this cross from the days of the Order's founder. They still do today.

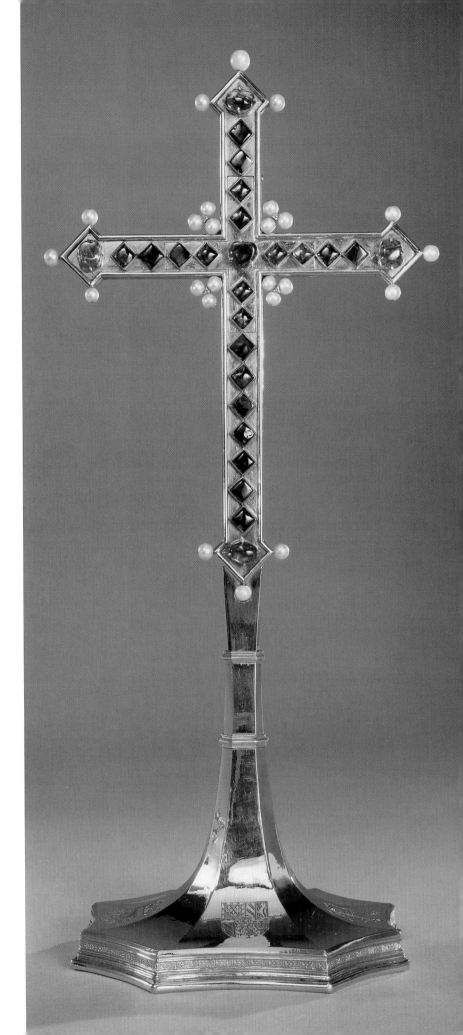

The Potence (Chain of Arms) for the Herald of the Order of the Golden Fleece
Netherlands, probably 1517.
Gold, enamel;
Circumference: outer 143 cm
Inner: 98.8 cm
(Dep. Prot. 4)

The Potence consists of a Collar (ornamental chain) of the Order and a Collar made up of 26 plates, each of which has two escutcheons bearing the arms of the Order's members. The sovereign had two slots. Charles V set the number of knights of the Order at 51.

Robes of a Knight of the Order of the Golden Fleece:
Mantle, Under-robe, Chaperon
Vienna, 1712 or 1755.
Velvet, silk, gold, silver and silk embroidery;
(Monturdepot Inv. No. TO 5)

These were the Emperor's robes.

**Mass Vestments of the Order of
the Golden Fleece**
Antependium (Frontal, altar cloth)
Detail: the Holy Trinity
Burgundian, between 1425 and 1440.
Strong linen background, gold
braided, embroidered with gold, silver
and silk thread, pearls, axinites;
330 cm long, 119 cm wide
(Inv. No. KK 18)

The embroidery depicts the Holy
Trinity with prophets and angels. The
way of representing the Trinity relates
to the Eucharist. The enthroned God
the Father shows his Son as a Man of
Sorrows. The Holy Ghost appears as
a dove on Jesus' shoulder. The picture
illustrates God's redemption through
Christ's sacrifice on the cross, which is
renewed in the Mass. The design was
ascribed to the Master of Flémalle
(Robert Campin (?), 1375-1444).

Mass Vestments of the Order of the Golden Fleece, Pluvial (Lady Cope)
Detail: Hood depicting the Virgin Mary
Detail: St Barbara
Burgundian, between 1425 and 1440.
Strong linen background, edged in red velvet and gold braid, gold and silver
thread, silk, pearls;
330 wide, 164 cm long
(Inv. No. KK 21)

Figures: hood: Mary; Orphreys: Apostles and Prophets; first row: Archangel
Gabriel with angels; next two rows: holy virgins, women and widows. Three of
such precious copes were made for Pontifical Vespers. The hoods at the back
formed a group picture, with Christ/God the Father in the middle, and Mary and
John the Baptist to either side. Their designs were again ascribed to the Master
of Flémalle.

Mass Vestments of the Order of the Golden Fleece, Chasuble Detail: the Three Apostles at Christ's Transfiguration
Burgundian, between 1425 and 1440. Strong linen background, edging of red velvet and gold braid, gold and silver thread, silk, pearls; 149.5 cm long, 135.5 cm wide (Inv. No. KK 14)

Figures: front: Christ's Baptism; back: Christ's Transfiguration; in three rows: angels. The chasuble is one of the last made of the vestments (in the 1430s). The great figures are again designed by the Master of Flémalle. The young Rogier van der Weyden (1399/1400-1464) may have contributed to the angels. The vestments in this whole set are among the most precious in the world.

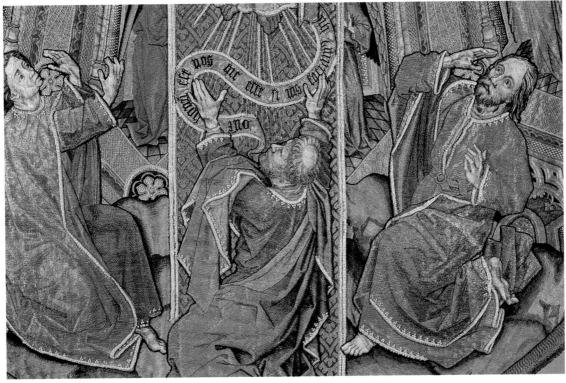

The Ecclesiastical Treasury

The ecclesiastical treasury consists mainly of liturgical vessels, paraments (vestments and ornaments) and precious relics, which were in use in the various imperial Court churches and chapels in Vienna, Schönbrunn, Laxenburg and Baden. Some of them are still in use today. First, we should mention the treasures in the Hofburg Chapel in Vienna. When the Emperor Joseph II began his reign in 1780, he put the Castle Chaplain in charge of the ecclesiastical treasury. He thereby created the assumption that the treasures from many different places would be united. As the Hofburg Chaplain had the rank of bishop, and in his chapel the most important ceremonies of the imperial Court took place, this Church naturally possessed particularly splendid altar vessels, decorations and monstrances. Its precious collection of paraments, mostly from the Baroque period, merits special attention.

Next, the visitor's attention will be drawn to the countless relics in their extraordinarily richly ornamented containers. They mainly date from the early 17th century, the Counter-Reformation period. These reliquaries were mostly made in Augsburg ateliers or in Munich, and in the imperial workshop set up by the Emperor Rudolf II in Prague, and probably also in Mantua. They are witness to the Hapsburg's piety and religious splendour, and to that of their Wittelsbach and Gonzaga relations, who were the fervent champions of the renewal of Catholicism in the Holy Roman Empire.

An enthusiastic patron of the cult of relics was the pious Empress Anna, the consort of the Emperor Matthias. She was also responsible for transferring some of these relics, which originally had been kept for the private devotion of their owners, to the treasury in the Capuchin Church in Vienna. In 1619 she also established the tombs of the Hapsburgs in the Capuchin crypt. There the relics served both as vehicles of faith and securities for a better life hereafter. In 1921 this 'Capuchin treasure' was returned to the safekeeping of the ecclesiastical treasury.

Finally, the countless devotional images of silver, ivory and bronze are worth particular attention. These include valuable gifts from Popes to the imperial Court.

Reproduction of the Mary Column at Am Hof in Vienna
Philipp Küsel (1642-1700).
Augsburg, about 1670/80.
Silver gilt, enamel, enamel painting, precious stones, pearls, glass, iron base; 129 cm high
(Inv. No. KK 882)

The precious ornament, encrusted with thousands of jewels (including 324 emeralds, 68 rubies and 452 amethysts) was commissioned by the Emperor Leopold I.

The So-called Monile
(Reliquary pendant) of the Emperor
Charlemagne
Prague (?), middle of 14th century.
Gold plate on wooden base, rock
crystal, gem stones, onyx cameo;
14.5 cm high, 9.3 cm wide
(Inv. No. 128)

According to the inscription on the
back, the Emperor Charles V carried
this relic of the cross with him in all
his battles and on all his journeys.
The beautiful cameo with the dancing
mënad is from the 2nd half of the 1st
century BC.

**Bag with Clasp, called King Stephen
of Hungary's Bag (d. 1038)**
Russian, 2nd half of 11th/12th century.
Gold and silk embroidery, silver gilt,
pearls, garnets, smoky quartz, glass;
15.5. cm high, 13.5 cm wide
(Inv. No. Kap. 186)

The ancient ascription is not historically
sound. The precious embroidery comes
from the early period of Russian art. The
pin, on which the smoky quartz hangs,
forms the bag's clasp.

THE ECCLESIASTICAL TREASURY

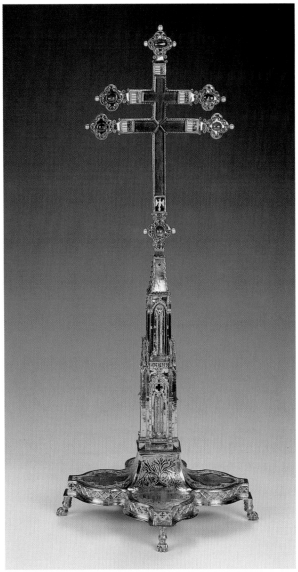

Mass Chalice
Hungary, about 1500.
Silver gilt, gem stones, axinites;
23.3 cm high
(Inv. No. B 10)

The chalice was in use in the Hofburg
chapel until 1854. There are similar
chalices in Slovakian churches and in
Siebenbürgen.

**Relic Cross of King Ludwig the
Great of Hungary**
Hungary, between 1370 and 1382.
Gold, silver gilt, enamel, precious
stones, pearls, rock crystal;
67.2 cm high
(Inv. No. D 251, 252)

Under the covering of rock crystal
there are several particles of Christ's
cross. On the ends of the cross there
are the allied arms of Hungary-Anjou
and below, the white eagle of Poland.
King Ludwig the Great (1326-82) of
the house of Anjou was also king of
Poland from 1370 onwards.

Winged House Altar
Matthias Walbaum (about
1554-1632).
Augsburg, about 1600.
Oak base, overlaid with ebony,
silver, partly gilt, copper
miniatures;
40.7 cm high, 18.5 cm wide
(Inv. No. D 179)

The house altar belonged to the
Emperor Matthias (1557-1619).
Centre: Adoration of the
shepherds; inner side of the
wings: Circumcision of Christ,
presentation in the Temple;
outer side of the wings:
Annunciation; on the sides of
the shrine: St George and St
Michael; top: three women at
the tomb of Christ, resurrection.

LEFT

Altarpiece for relics
Matthias Walbaum (about
1554-1632).
Augsburg, about 1600/05.
Oak base, overlaid with ebony.
hardwood stained black, silver,
partly gilt;
49 cm high, 28.8 cm wide
(Inv. No. D 89)

The Ostensory follows larger
altars in its design. The central
part contains the relics of various
saints in 17 compartments. The
figures of Caritas (Charity) and
Temperantia (Temperance) stand
on consoles on the left, and
Fides (Faith) and Spes (Hope)
stand on consoles on the right.

**Ostensory with a Thorn from Christ's Crown
of Thorns and with Relics of Various Saints,
Detail: figure on the top**
Mantua, 1592.
Oak base, overlaid with ebony, gold, partly
enamelled, silver gilt, diamonds, rubies,
emeralds, pearls, rock crystal;
50.4 cm high
(Inv. No. D 21)

The crowning female figure in armour, carved like
a jewel, holds a chalice in her left hand and lays her
right hand on the cross. She is an allegory for
militant faith.

Tempietto with relics of Christ
Mantua, end of 16th century.
Hard wood, overlaid with ebony, gold enamelled,
silver, diamonds, garnets, pearls, rock crystal;
49 cm high
(Inv. No. D 23)

The rock crystal vase hanging between pillars was
believed to contain drops of Christ's blood. Six
other passion relics are kept in the roof area. In the
base there is a linen cloth soaked in Christ's blood.

Reliquary of St Elizabeth
Augsburg, beginning of 17th century.
Hardwood, overlaid with ebony, silver,
partly gilt and enamelled, rubies, pearls,
silk, gold braid, wax;
31 x 30.4 x 19 cm
(Inv. No. D 48)

Above the relic, which is half the shin bone
of St Elizabeth of Thuringia (1207-31),
there is a wax model of St Elizabeth feeding
the poor.

Altarpiece with Rock Crystal Carving
Munich, end of 16th century, after a design by
Christoph Schwarz (1548-92).
Hardwood, overlaid with ebony, rock crystal,
gold foil, silver, almandine;
25.5 x 16.5 cm
(Inv. No. Kap. 181)

**Two Reliquaries with Half Figures
of St Valerian and St Tiburtius in Wax**
Munich, beginning of 17th century, after
designs by Hans Krumper (1570-1643).
Wax, textiles, pearls, hardwood, overlaid
with ebony, gold enamelled, bronze gilt;
36 cm high, 22.5 cm wide
(Inv. Nos. D 70, D 71)

Originally the putti offered the saints laurel wreaths.
The relics in the boxes were exchanged after 1780
for relics of St Mauritius and St Crispin.

Two Feather Mosaic Pictures showing Christ and Mary
Juan Baptista Cuiris Michoacán (Pátzcuaro) Mexico, about 1550-80.
Humming bird and parrot feathers on paper background, wood;
25.4 x 18.2 cm, with frames: 38 x 24.3 cm
(Inv. Nos. Kap 321, Kap 322)

These two pieces are the only preserved signed feather mosaic pictures. They were produced in the craft tradition of the Tarasks in workshops set up by Vasco de Quiroga (1537-56), the first bishop of the province of Michoacán.

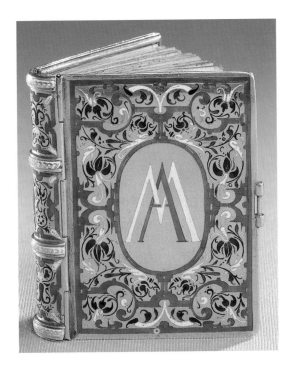

Prayer Book of Ferdinand II (1578-1637)
Augsburg (?), 1590.
Gold enamelled, parchment with gilt edging;
6 x 4.8 cm, page size 5.6 x 4.4 cm
(Inv. No. D 27)

The Emperor-to-be received the book from his parents, when he went to the Jesuit school in Ingolstadt in 1590.

Enthroned Madonna with Child, being Worshipped by Angels. Silver Relief from an Altar
Augsburg, about 1600.
Silver, partly gilt, almandine;
33 cm high, 25 cm wide
(Inv. No. Kap. 2089

Relic Casket
Venice (?), 3rd quarter of
16th century.
Wood, stained black and
gilded, sardonyx, lapis lazuli,
water colour on parchment;
26 x 48 x 31 cm
(Inv. No. D 185)

The inside lid is inlaid with lapis
lazuli platelets; in the centre there
is a miniature by Joris Hoefnagel
(1542-1600) showing Christ's
ascension into heaven.

Madonna Standing on the Crescent Moon
Figure: Christoph Lencker (about 1556-1613).
Base: Jeremias I Wildt (d. 1608).
Augsburg, about 1608-13.
Silver, partly gilt; 42.5 cm high, 19 cm wide,
13 cm deep
(Inv. No. Kap 21)

According to the inscription, the relics in the base
are particles of Mary's veil. The statue's shape recalls
Hubert Gerhard's (1593) famous statue of Mary on a
column in Munich, which stood on the high altar of
the Frauenkirche (Lady Church) until 1620.

St Joseph
Augsburg, about 1620/25.
Base with artist's sign of Hans Jakob I
Bachmann (active 1598-1651).
Silver, partly gilt;
40.5 cm high, 20 cm wide, 14.5 cm deep
(Inv. No. Kap 22)

Companion piece to the Madonna
statuette. The figure shows Joseph as
a wandering carpenter with his tools.
According to the inscription, the relic
in the base is part of St Joseph's cloak,
in which he wrapped Jesus at his birth.

Relic House Altar
Workshop of Miseroni, Milan,
beginning of 17th century.
Hardwood base, overlaid with ebony,
jasper, agate, rock crystal, gold
enamelled, diamonds, rubies, pearls;
44.5 cm high, 26 cm wide
(Inv. No. Kap. 221)

Gift from Duke Charles Emanuel
of Savoy (1562/80-1630) to the
Empress Anna (wife of Emperor
Matthias) between 1611 and 1618.
In the top-piece, behind rock
crystal, there is a thorn from
Christ's crown of thorns. The agate
crucifix in the green jasper niche is
flanked by the gold-enamelled
figures of Mary and John.

Two Relic Monstrances
Ottavio Miseroni (1567-1624).
Prague, about 1620.
Agate, jasper, lapis lazuli,
diamonds, rubies, pearls, gold
enamelled, silver gilt;
30 or 33.5 cm high, 19 cm wide
(Inv. Nos. Kap. 219, Kap 220)

The medallions in the centre are
commessi reliefs (put together from
an assembly of hard stones). One
portrays the Madonna and Child;
the other shows St Anna together
with the Madonna and Child.
Both bear the signature of Ottavio
Miseroni. The relics in the base of
the ëdicule, are of 'our dear Lady's
shift' in one, and a scrap of St
Anna's dress in the other. The
Empress Anna ordered the two
reliquaries to be made in her will
of 10.11.1618.

Crucifix
Leonhard Kern (1588-1662)
Swabian, about 1625/1630.
Wood, black stained, and walnut (?)
Height of the body to the top of
the head 53.6 cm;
Width of spread arms 53.3 cm
(Inv. No. E 109)

The unusually monumental body,
whose full frontal depiction recalls
high Renaissance works of the early
16th century, was regarded for a
long time as the work of Albrecht
Dürer. This happened in the
engraving of it by Franciscus von
de Steen after Nicolas van Hoy in
about 1650. Thus the crucifix
shows Leonhard Kern to have been
one of the most important
protagonists of the 'Dürer
Renaissance' in the first half of the
16th century.

Crucifixion Group
South German, 1st quarter of 17th century.
Bronze, light brown patina, wood;
height of crucifix 101.5 cm
(Inv. No. E 34)

The Christ figure is of the type developed in
the late 1580s by Giambologna in Florence,
which spread widely throughout Italy.
However, the figures of Mary, John and
Mary Magdalene standing under the cross
are in the tradition of Munich sculpture
around 1600. So we can assume the
crucifixion group originated in this vicinity.

Ostensory with a Nail from Christ's Cross
Augsburg (?), mid-17th century.
Gold, partly enamelled, silver gilt, brass painted, iron, emeralds, sapphires, topaz,
aquamarine, amethysts, turquoise, hyacinth, rock crystal, garnets, pearls and glass;
79.6 cm high
(Inv. No. D 62)

The almond shaped holder displays the nail that was said to have been nailed into Christ's right hand
on the cross. Later the Emperor Constantine the Great had this nail worked into his helmet. At least
this is stated by a document of Pope Innocent II (1130-1143), whose seal can be seen beside the nail.
The nail's healing power was so highly prized that visitors used to rub their rosaries on the capsule,
hoping that some of the power would rub off on them.

Relic Altarpiece with a Thorn from Christ's Crown of Thorns
Milan (?), about 1660/1680.
Hardwood overlaid with ebony, gold enamel, silver gilt, brass gilt,
diamonds precious stones, gem stones, pearls, axinites, glass beads;
70 cm high, base 12 cm high
(Inv. No. D 59)

The altarpiece's decoration combines a number of individual figures to give
a joint impression of great richness. A crowned L and the inscription 'ERIT
UNICA MIHI' ('This shall belong to me alone') on the back of the flower
vase on the top-piece relate to the Emperor Leopold I.

Reliquary with a Particle of Christ's Cross, the so-called Monstrance of the Order of the Starry Cross
Vienna or Augsburg, about 1668.
Gold, silver gilt and enamelled.
diamonds, chrysoliths, garnets,
amethysts, agates, cornelians;
53.5 cm high
(Inv. No. D 25)

This particle of the cross remained miraculously unharmed in a fire in the Hofburg in 1668. It was in the possession of the Empress Dowager Eleonora Gonzaga at the time. That was the occasion for the creation of this reliquary and the foundation of the Order of the Starry Cross, the principal Ladies' Order of the House of Austria.

Lamenting and Anointing of Christ
Leonhard Kern (1588-1662)
about 1615/20.
Ivory on ebony in a wooden case under glass;
24.5 cm high, 40.2 cm wide
(Inv. No. D 198)

The strong Italian influence and the additive character of the composition suggest an early work by this artist, who spent some years studying and travelling in Italy.

Allegory on the Death of Emperor Ferdinand III
Daniel Neuberger (1621-80)
Vienna, about 1660.
Wax modelling, shimmering, coloured sand,
in an ebony box under glass;
36.5 cm high, 46.5 cm wide
(Inv. No. Kap. 244)

There is an hour glass beside the Emperor, who died in 1657. Nine skeletons dance round him in a dance of death. The hour glass is a warning that mortality does not spare even emperors. But a hand appearing from above carries a ribbon inscribed with the word 'VIVIT' (he lives), as a comforting reminder of eternal life.

Veronica's Handkerchief (the Sudarium)
Frame: Rome 1617, and Vienna, about 1721 (?)
Linen, ebony, silver partly gilt, copper gilt, mother of pearl, onyx cameos, ivory; 58.5 cm high, 48.4 cm wide
(Inv. No. D 108)

The Sudarium originated from Rome and was given as a present by Princess Savelli to the Emperor Charles VI in 1720. As there are several such relics, people believed that Veronica folded the cloth in three, so that Christ's blood and sweat soaked through to all three layers of material. The relic was regarded as 'one of the most remarkable objects in the imperial ecclesiastical treasury and the imperial residence in Vienna'.

Tabernacle with Ostensory for a Particle of Christ's Cross
Giovanni Giardini da Forlç (1646-1721) and Pietro Paolo Gelpi (1664-1751), Rome 1711.
Porphyry, bronze gilt, silver gilt, rock crystal, diamonds, rubies axinites; 122 cm high, 74 cm wide, 27 cm deep
(Inv. No. D 77)

This was a gift of Pope Clement XI to King Charles III of Spain, who later became the Emperor Charles VI. The Pope gave it to Charles when he was in Milan on his way to his coronation in Germany. Giardini is one of the most important decorative sculptors of the Roman Baroque period.

The Meeting of Pope Leo the Great
with Attila King of the Huns

Ercole Ferrata (1610-86) after Alessandro Algardi (1598-1654),
Rome, about 1660.
Bronze fired gilt, Frame: Bronze, copper silver;
98 cm high, 59.5 cm wide
(Inv. No. D 164)

Alessandro Algardi used this theme between 1646 and 1653 for a
colossal marble relief in St Peter's in Rome. The work made his
international reputation. The reduced size versions, made after
Algardi's death by Ercole Ferrata, were used by the Pope as gifts
to European courts.

Meissen Altar Set

Johann Joachim Kaendler (1706-75)
Meissen, about 1737/1741.
Porcelain, partly gilt, burnt-in colours
Candle sticks: bronze gilt
Cross on stand: 86.3 cm high
(Inv. Nos. KK 7078-7111)

Kaendler, the most important modeller at the Meissen porcelain
manufactory, created the models for the statuettes after the manner
of the monumental series of apostles in the basilica of St John
Lateran in Rome. The set was a present from August II of Saxony
to his mother-in-law, the Empress Dowager Wilhelmine Amalia of
Braunschweig-Lüneburg.

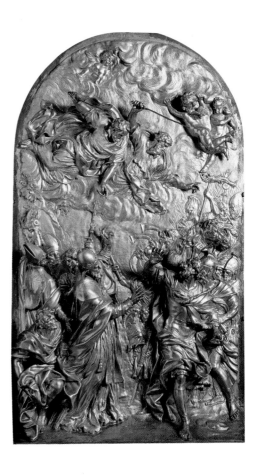

Pacificale
Johann Baptist Känischbauer von Hohenried (1668-1739), Vienna, 1726.
Gold, partly enamelled, rock crystal, diamonds, rubies, pearls, axinites, silver gilt;
25.3 cm high
(Inv. No. D 39)

Above the symbols of the four evangelists rests the rock crystal globe containing a particle of
Christ's cross. Above that stands the Redeemer with streaming halo. He is represented as the
timeless Christ Child, who triumphs over the cross and becomes ruler of the world through his
sacrifice. The design for this reliquary was probably a drawing by the great Austrian Baroque
architect, Johann Bernhard Fischer von Erlach.

**Monstrance with a Figure of Mary as
Holder for the Host**
Zacharias Feil
(active 1695-1742).
Vienna, 1701.
Silver, partly gilt, gem stones,
rock crystal, pearls, glass;
66 cm high
(Inv. No. Kap. 88)

The open body of the Mother of God is
designed to enclose the Host, in which
Christ is present. This symbolically
expresses Mary's contribution, as God's
mother, to the redemption of humanity
in the Eucharist.

Monstrance
Zacharias Friedrich Würth
(active 1740-1760),
Vienna 1760
Silver gilt, partly enamelled; diamonds,
precious stones, gem stones, pearls;
71.5 cm high
(Inv. No. B 30)

The Trinity is represented through God
the Father, the dove of the Holy Ghost
and Christ present in the Host. The lamb
symbolises Christ's sacrificial death. Vine
leaves and grapes are eucharistic symbols.

Three Mass Chalices
Maker unknown, Josef M. Huber, Josef Moser,
Vienna, 1747, 1767, 1775.
Silver gilt, enamel painting, diamonds
precious stones, gem stones;
29.4 cm; 30 cm; 27.2 cm high
(Inv. Nos. B 7, B 4, B 8)

The three chalices are magnificent examples of
the extraordinary quality of work produced by
Vienna goldsmiths from the Rococo to the
Early Classical period.

Crucifix
Austria (?), about 1710/20.
Ivory, axinite, hardwood stained black;
Total height: 87.5 cm
(Inv. No. E 46)

Great technical skill and expressiveness
distinguish this masterpiece by a still
unknown virtuoso sculptor.

Relic Busts of St John, St Matthias, St John the Baptist and St Andrew
Josef Moser (1715-1801) and Workshop, Vienna, before 1758.
Silver, bronze gilt and silvered; 33, 35, 31, 33 cm high
(Inv. Nos. D 87, D 20, D 3, D 99)

The busts belong to a series of 14. They were probably commissioned by the Empress Maria Theresia.

Christ as the Man of Sorrows
Paul Egell (1691-1752), Mannheim, about 1730/35.
Ivory in hardwood frame; 17.7 cm high, 13.7 cm wide
(Inv. No. KK 3660)

Here all the possibilities of ivory carving are exploited in the subtlest way. Delicacy of form and a soft surface carving, giving the effect of half shadow, contrast with the graphic elements of the fully elaborated sculptural details.

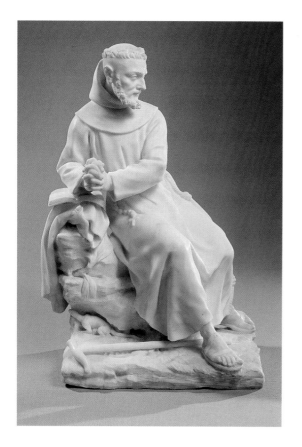

St Francis of Assisi
St Teresa of Avila
Laurent Delvaux (1696-1778)
Nivelles, 1765.
Carrara marble;
50 cm high
(Inv. Nos. D 98 and D 94)

The saints are the name patrons
of the Emperor Franz I and the
Empress Maria Theresia. The two
statuettes were commissioned by
the Empress.

Silver Frame with a Picture of
St Antony of Padua
Frame: Josef Moser (1715-1801),
Vienna, 1747.
Picture: Circle of Franciabigio, Florence,
beginning of 16th century.
Silver on wood;
100 cm high, 102 cm wide
(Inv. No. D 166)

The clearly architectonic structure of the frame,
which continued into the Rococo period, is
characteristic of Vienna gold and silver work.

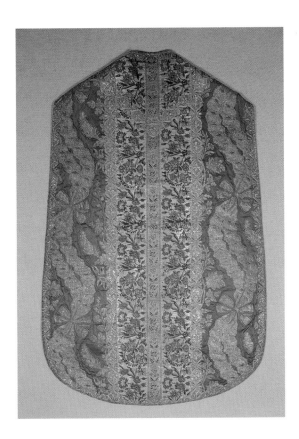

Red Chasuble
Vienna, 3rd quarter of 18th century.
European and Persian silk weave
2nd half of 17th century, the orphrey band
is of finest Persian silk lamé, stitched with
gold and coloured, partly lanced silk, silver
embroidery;
107 cm high, 72 cm wide
(Inv. No. A 108)

Coral Chasuble
Italian, 1st half of 18th century.
Gold embroidery with corals on silver lamé;
106 cm high, 72 cm wide
(Inv. No. A 51)

Violet Chasuble
Vienna, 1st half of 18th century.
Silk damask, stitched in flat and frisé silver and
coloured silk, French, about 1710/20. Gold braid;
111 cm high, 77 cm wide
(Inv. No. A 140)

The large stock of precious Mass vestments was largely
the result of the rich endowments by the Emperor
Charles VI and his wife Elizabeth Christine, as well as
their daughter Maria Theresia. Often clothes from the
imperial wardrobe were re-worked.

Rulers of the Holy Roman Empire, the Empire of Austria, Spain and Burgundy

Holy Roman Empire

The rulers of the house of Hapsburg/Hapsburg-Lorraine are in Roman type, those of other dynasties are in italics.

King Rudolf I of Hapsburg (ruled 1273-1291)
King Adolf of Nassau (ruled 1292-1298)
King Albrecht I (ruled 1298-1308)
Emperor Henry VII (ruled 1308-1313)
Frederick the Fair (died 1330)
Emperor Ludwig IV, the Bavarian (ruled 1314-1347)
Emperor Charles IV (ruled 1347-1378)
King Wenceslaus (ruled 1378-1400)
King Rupert of the Palatinate (ruled 1400-1410)
King Jobst of Moravia (ruled 1410-1411)
Emperor Sigismund (ruled 1411-1437)
King Albrecht II (ruled 1438-1439)
Emperor Frederick III (ruled 1440-1493)
Emperor Maximilian I (ruled 1493-1519)
Emperor Charles V (ruled 1519-1556)
Emperor Ferdinand I (ruled 1556-1564)
Emperor Maximilian II (ruled 1564-1576)
Emperor Rudolf II (ruled 1576-1612)
Emperor Matthias (ruled 1612-1619)
Emperor Ferdinand II (ruled 1619-1637)
Emperor Ferdinand III (ruled 1637-1657)
Emperor Leopold I (ruled 1658-1705)
King Ferdinand IV (died 1683)
Emperor Joseph I (ruled 1705-1711)
Emperor Charles VI (ruled 1711-1740)
Emperor Charles VII (ruled 1742-1745)
Emperor Franz I (ruled 1745-1765)
Emperor Joseph II (ruled 1765-1790)
Emperor Leopold II (ruled 1790-1792)
Emperor Franz II (ruled 1792-1806)

Empire of Austria

Emperor Franz I (ruled 1804-1835)
 [Franz II as Roman Emperor]
Emperor Ferdinand I (ruled 1835-1848)
Emperor Franz Joseph I (ruled 1848-1916)
Emperor Charles I (ruled 1916-1918)

The Older Spanish Line of the House of Hapsburg

Emperor Charles V (ruled 1516-1556)
 [Charles I as King of Spain]
King Philip II (ruled 1556-1598)
King Philip III (ruled 1598-1621)
King Philip IV (ruled 1621-1665)
King Charles II (ruled 1665-1700)

Dukes of Burgundy

Duke Philip the Bold of Burgundy
 (ruled 1363-1404)
Duke John the Fearless of Burgundy
 (ruled 1404-1419)
Duke Philip the Good of Burgundy
 (ruled 1419-1467)
Duke Charles the Bold Burgundy
 (ruled 1467-1477)
Duchess Maria of Burgundy
 (ruled 1477-1482)
 married Emperor Maximilian I